Book of Stories

Caleb Gattegno

Educational Solutions Worldwide Inc.

Educational Solutions Worldwide Inc.
2nd Floor 99 University Place, New York, N.Y. 10003-4555
www.EducationalSolutions.com

1

- *at sunset pat and pam went in with sam*

- *tim and tom were still on the sand*

- *sam sat on a step and pam on a mat*

- *pat was upset because she lost ten stamps*

- *the sand was full of wet lumps but tim and tom sat on them*

- *mom and dad told them to run in as it was dinner time*

2

- in the family there are mom and dad and five of us, sam, pam, tom, pat, and tim

- sam is up first, tim last

- sam has a bed and tim and tom a bunk

- pam and pat have a room on the first floor

- pat is tall and tim is small

- tom is as tall as pam but pam is older

- sam is nine and tim is five, tom is seven

- sam is the oldest and his sisters and brothers love him very much

3

- pat has a pet, it is fat and sits on mom's lap

- sam has a thin and dull cat found on the rocks, pat's cat is not his friend

- sam's cat wants to go out, pat's cat wants to stay in

- when sam's cat is out, pat's cat starts to jump around the house and to drink and eat

- when sam's cat is back, pat's cat hides in mom's lap

- pam, tom, and tim have no pets

4

- we have a tent in the garden

- dad set it up and we all helped him

- we put in it two camp beds, a table and three chairs, a few mats, and some other things

- when it is warm we may sleep in the tent

- sam always takes one of the camp beds and the other is for one of us or for daddy

- sam has many books and likes to read late, but in the tent he reads out loud for all of us

5

- *dad tells us stories, in the house, in the tent, or on the sand*

- *we love his stories, they are fun*

- *mom gives us all we need, takes us shopping with her and sometimes lets us help her in the kitchen*

- *mom often asks pam and pat to clean the house with her*

- *tom is also eager to help but tim prefers to go out with sam*

6

- sam and tim went to the market, mom sent sam to buy carrots

- at the market there was a basket full of apples

- a red apple from the top rolled down and fell in the gutter

- tim picked it up and handed it to the man with the basket but the man gave it to him

- tim said thank you, washed the apple under the tap, and ate it all

- sam said nothing

- he bought carrots and also two good red apples and bit into one of them

- tim asked him for the other, but sam pretended he had not heard him and when he finished the first apple started eating the second

- tim looked at him with his eyes wide open and soon started crying

- when they reached home, tim was still crying and mom asked him why

- tim said: sam bought two apples and ate them both

- sam said: did you not eat a red apple at the market, one like the ones I ate

- yes, but you ate two and I ate only one

- if I had given you one, you would have eaten two and I one, is that better

- but the one I ate, said tim, the man gave to me, not to you

- and who bought the two red apples, you or me

- tim was puzzled and stopped crying, he could not understand what sam was saying or why

7

- dad hired two ponies for us to ride at the zoo

- sam and pat went first with the two men and dad took those of us left to look at the animals

- there were a number of kangaroos some with their little ones in their pouches

- and in the next enclosure there were zebras with their black and white stripes

- as we were looking at them, the ponies returned and tim and tom replaced sam and pat

- dad took us to the other side of the path to a cage full of parrots

- they were of all colors and many could talk

- some said: good morning, big boy, others said: hello, come again, and still others said such funny things as: be careful of the water or open your umbrella

- we laughed a lot with the parrots but we could not hear them very well when they all talked together

- next to the parrots was an open air enclosure with flamingoes, what beautiful feathers they had, and many were standing only on one leg for some time

- the ponies returned but I did not want to go alone and dad was too big to go with me, sam in a moment replaced tom on one and I was now happy to go

- we went on looking at the animals in the zoo and enjoyed every minute of it

- when we reached home we were very hungry and ate all mother had prepared for us

8

- as sam's cat did not come back that night he asked mom whether he could go to the market to try to find him, she said that he could but he should not be late

- on his way he stopped at a site where a man was working and some other men were looking at him

- the man down there was using a pneumatic drill to break a big lump of rock into pieces

- the man was very strong and worked very hard as the rock was huge and not easy to cut

- sam looked at his arms and thought, I would like to be as strong as he and have a pneumatic drill to handle

- the people standing left one by one and sam was alone looking at him, fascinated

- he did not know how long he had stayed there forgetting his cat and his promise to mom, so he went home at once

- he was greeted there by the cries of all the others: why did you go to look for him, when he knew the way home so well

- sam said nothing about the man with the pneumatic drill and showed how pleased he was to have found his cat back at home

9

- dad took the three boys to town

- they went by bus as it was easier that way

- sam and tim sat together and dad and tom behind them

- from the window they could see the route and they noted that between their home and the town there was a long stretch of lovely country

- there were trees of all sorts and sizes with barks of different colors and leaves of different shapes, fields that were green or gold, and one covered with yellow flowers

- they saw farms and villages in the distance and dad had to tell them the name of every place

- the countryside became hilly and the bus slowed down every time it went up but also every time it went down

- they could feel their bodies press against the seat as they went up and they sometimes had to hold onto the arm when going down

- at a stop two elderly ladies got on, there were no vacant seats, so sam and tim jumped to their feet and told the ladies to take their seats

- the ladies sat down thanking sam and tim who were pleased and embarrassed because people were looking at them

- tom looked at them and his eyes were saying I am still on my seat and do not need to hang on as you do

- one of the ladies asked tim to sit on her lap, he was too proud to accept though he would have liked to go on looking through the window but, like sam, he kept standing till they reached their destination

10

- mom took the two girls to visit aunt rachel

- aunt rachel is mom's own aunt, she is seventy-five and always as alert as a young woman

- we love to go to see her because she is so kind and mom loves her so dearly

- *aunt rachel has hands like those of fairies for she can knit most complicated patterns in several colors and makes beautiful garments*

- *she has also done embroidery, laces, and all sorts of fine handwork that we never see in stores nowadays*

- *to visit her is to hear her tell you many things of the past when ladies were shown how to make beautiful things rather than buy them*

- *pam and pat love to look at the collection of embroidered skirts, blouses, and dresses and hear time and again the story of each, one dress was finished sixty years ago when she and mom's mother held its train at the wedding of one of their cousins*

- *for pam and pat all these stories of aunt rachel are fairy stories because they never see around them what she talks about, but they believe her when she tells them that she was there when this or that happened and, when they go home, mom explains what she can*

- *aunt rachel wants to see the boys but they are not so interested in clothes and they prefer to go to town with dad when mom goes to visit her*

- *mom always invites aunt rachel to spend a day at her house but she thinks it better to stay at home and use her time in making something, she is happy that way*

11

- *in the night tim cried suddenly and woke up dad and mom who went to him at once*

- *his cries were like those of someone very frightened and calling for help*

- *mom took him in her arms and kissed him on his brow and comforted him as best she could*

- *but tim was sobbing and still under the impression of his bad dream*

- *dad asked him what he saw in his dream but tim could not tell him, he only said that he saw something awful that was coming nearer and nearer to him*

- *mom knew that they could do nothing now to make him not dream but their love made him safe and go to sleep again in her arms*

- *perhaps he ate too much this evening, said dad, or perhaps he jumped too much after his dinner and could not digest it well, these bad dreams often come because of that and we should be careful not to let them go to bed too soon after a big dinner*

- *mom agreed*

- sam had vaguely heard tim cry and the next morning he asked mom if he had

- he too had a dream that was not pleasant and felt his stomach aching but he did not cry as he was a big boy

- tom asked tim to tell him what he had dreamed but tim could say nothing, he even forgot that he had cried and had been taken into mother's arms

- pam and pat wanted to know how dreams come about, but no one could answer except sam who said that dreams were in the eyes and when we close them we can still see what we want

- during the night we sleep with our eyes closed but we can see things and these are our dreams

- dad smiled very pleased

12

- the children are at school five days a week, tim only in the mornings

- mom goes to get him at noon but in the morning sam takes him to school

- sam does not play with tom when he is at school since tom is two years younger, nor does pam play with pat

- they only play together at home and when the family goes to the country

- they prefer it when they are together as they have always been, but at school you cannot play with your brothers and sisters, you must play with your classmates

- some of them are tough and rough and sam has to defend himself as they fight with everybody all the time

- one day sam came home with a pain in his chest because a rough boy had punched him in the ribs with all his strength

- mom was very sorry for sam and very annoyed with that boy

- she wanted to call the teacher but sam said she must not

- he would show him the next day that he too could be tough

- mom was not pleased at the idea but she agreed with sam that he should not let others bully him and that it was better for the children to manage their own affairs in their own way

13

- pam has a teacher she loves very much

- miss dunn is her name and every day pam has something to tell about her at home

- first she tells about her dresses, her shoes, her belt when she has one, her handbag, and her hat when she brings one to school

- then she tells of her sweet voice and how nicely she talks to everyone

- sometimes she even tells of the lessons

- pam likes the music lessons and movement

- miss dunn plays the piano and the flute

- when they can use the music room, miss dunn plays the piano, otherwise she uses her own flute

- the children sing or dance according to the tune played and now they know so many that each pupil in the class can sing three different songs while the others hum the tunes

- when miss dunn plays tunes that have no words, she lets the pupils move as they feel, each in their own way

- when she stops playing they must keep still until she starts playing again

- the pupils love this type of game and always try new things

- pam showed everyone today what happened in these lessons and pat learned to play with her

- mom told them that they can play this game at home

- she will put a record on and when she stops it everyone must remain still as a statue

- this game was such fun that for six months they played it for a while every day

- miss dunn would be pleased if she knew but pam does not want to tell her yet

14

- *in the kitchen mom was cooking dinner.*

- *sam went to her and said, "may I help in any way?"*

- *"it is kind of you to offer, but I have already peeled the potatoes and washed the salad, what do you think you can do?"*

- *"I do not know, tell me what we will have for our dinner and I may find something to do."*

- *"all right, I am preparing a dish you all like, eggs and potatoes cooked in the oven as well as green salad with french dressing."*

- *"have you prepared the eggs and the dressing?" asked sam.*

- *"not yet," said mom.*

- *"well, may I prepare them?"*

- *"do you know how to do it?"*

- *"I put water in the saucepan and place it on the stove, turn the knob round to light the gas, and when the water boils I put the eggs in it and let them stay for a while."*

- *"good boy,"* said mother, *"go ahead and prepare the eggs."*

- while sam was doing that, mother asked him, *"do you know how to prepare a french dressing for the salad?"*

- sam said *"I know that you put in oil and vinegar, salt and pepper, but I do not know how much of each nor in what order."*

- *"well, we shall do it together when we have finished what we are doing."*

- at that moment pam and pat came in and asked mother whether they could help.

- mother replied that sam had already offered to do so and she had accepted and now two more people in the kitchen would be too many, *"why not set the table instead?"* asked mother.

- pat and pam preferred to help with the cooking rather than set the table, and they suggested that sam should set the table while they prepared the dressing.

- sam said sharply, *"no, you set the table or go out to play, I am mother's assistant in the kitchen today."*

- *"all right, we will go out to play and you set the table too, sam."*

- *"I do not mind, but you certainly are mean."*

- *when they were alone in the kitchen mother asked sam if he too was not mean to have refused to give his place to his sisters.*

- *sam did not see why, but became silent while waiting for his mother to finish and help him prepare the dressing.*

15

- tim went to the shoe store with dad to buy a new pair of shoes.

-his last pair had been black and the pair before that, brown.

- both pairs were no longer good but tim wanted to know which pair he was replacing, the brown or the black.

- dad did not want to waste much time at the store as he had an appointment and told the salesperson to quickly find a good pair that would last for some time.

- tim had not yet made up his mind about the color.

- the salesperson was already trying two or three pairs on him.

- he only asked him, "is this all right? does it fit? does it hurt?"

- tim did not want to answer, he first wanted to know which pair he was to replace and only then to try on shoes of that color and only then answer the salesperson.

- but dad was in a hurry and did not listen to tim asking him, "which pair am I replacing?"

- "I do not want to have two black pairs or two brown pairs."

- dad and the salesperson only asked the same questions about fitting and hurting and never got an answer from tim, who in turn never got an answer from dad about which pair he was replacing.

- dad got cross after some time and said to the salesperson, "I am sorry to have bothered you, I'll send him with his mother tomorrow."

- he told tim, "you are so awkward and unreasonable, I hope that you will not drive your mother as crazy as you do me, I wasted so much time with you!"

- tim thought, "first I shall find out which pair I am replacing and all will be easy with dad or mom."

16

- mom had visitors today, a friend and her baby daughter uma who was brought in her car-bed.

- pam was rocking the little baby in her bed.

- the baby was quiet but not yet asleep.

- pat came in excited and talking loudly, "pam come and see this lovely butterfly."

- pam said sharply, "keep quiet, don't you see that I am trying to help uma sleep?"

- uma became interested in the two voices and opened her half-closed eyes to have a better look at the two persons near her.

- pat put her hand to her mouth and looked ashamed.

- pam looked cross but was also interested in what pat came to tell her.

- pam said to pat, "where is the lovely butterfly?"

- "in one of the roses," said pat.

- "well, you rock uma's bed while I go out to see it, try to make her go to sleep."

- pam went out and pat sat on the stool and started to rock the bed, uma looked at her and smiled, pleased to see her so near now.

- pat looked at uma, but was thinking of the lovely butterflies that were dancing in the garden in the sun.

- she wished she were out too.

-uma understood her wish and shut her eyes as if she were asleep.

- pat stopped rocking her, looked at her, got up and left the room on tiptoe to run to the garden to be with pam and the exciting butterflies.

- uma opened her eyes, smiled, and quietly satisfied, fell into a deep sleep.

17

- *every day when they came back from school the four older children would play outside in the garden if it was pleasant and indoors when it was raining or too cold.*

- *tim would join them and often he would spoil the games as he could not do what sam or pam could easily do.*

- *but after one hour mother would call them in to give them a snack.*

- *on the table there would be butter and margarine, cups of milk, toasted bread, cookies, jams, cheese sanswiches, tomatoes, and every day something extra that was different.*

- *the children always looked forward to that extra treat because not all of them had the same tastes and mother tried hard to satisfy everyone.*

- *one day she would cook liver, but tom does not touch it.*

- *another day she would bring fresh fish and seafood but sam would turn his face away and eat lots of slices of bread with butter and jam instead.*

- *yet another day mother would have roast chicken prepared but pam likes it only when it has been boiled and then cooked in the oven with potatoes.*

- pat has developed an aversion for cold meat and tim is unsure of many dishes.

- mother is very patient and always tries to change the way she prepares her meals and puts them on the table and always tries to convince everyone that if they taste her dish they will like it at once.

- but they rarely try and rarely does mom see everyone eat everything she prepares.

- eggs with potatoes and green salads with french dressing they all like, but mom cannot give them the same food every day.

- she must have a change even if one or two do not eat what she gives them.

18

- *the other day a truck stopped at the door and a big cardboard box was brought in.*

- *the man asked mom to sign a paper and then he left.*

- *"what is there in this box?" asked pat and tom at the same time.*

- *mom said, "I do not know, daddy ordered it and did not tell me."*

- *"can't you open it and let us see?"*

- *"no" said mother, "it is dad's order and he must be here to open it and see if he wants it."*

- *mom left the entrance hall and went to the kitchen.*

- *the five children stood in front of the closed box and were very curious.*

- *sam pushed it a little and saw how light it was.*

- *"such a big box and so light, what can be inside?"*

- they all started guessing: "not a washing machine," said pam, "not a refrigerator," said sam, "not a stove," said pat, as all of them remembered that these arrived in crates of the same size as this carton.

- "could it be a rug?" asked tim.

- they all stopped talking, thinking whether it was possible.

- sam said "let us roll up the rug in the front room and see if it is as light as this carton."

- they rolled the rug but the five of them could barely lift it.

- they unrolled the rug and put everything as it was.

- tom said, "let us go around the house and see everything we have and think of it as put into a cardboard box."

- "good idea," said sam, "let us go."

- they looked at chairs, armchairs, cupboards, blankets, sheets, curtains, and most of the things around but none would fit the two things they knew about the box, its size and its weight.

- while they were still studying the items in the house, dad came in and said, "oh! this wretched thing has arrived at last."

- they all ran to him and asked together, "what is that wretched thing?"

- "it is a surprise for you: a flamingo like the one you saw at the zoo the other day, but this one is stuffed with foam rubber."

- "you can let it stand behind the door so that you look at it when you go in and out "

- "do you like the idea?"

- they did like it and were surprised but they were still more surprised that no one thought of it, now they could see that a flamingo stuffed with foam rubber would be just that height and that weight.

- "can we open the box now?" asked pam.

- "you must be very careful otherwise you may cut into the feathers of the bird."

- with great care they found a place to insert a knife and cut the wrappings.

- after a few minutes they brought out of the box the pinkish bird standing on one leg just like the ones they had seen at the zoo.

- *they looked and looked, went round and round it, not daring to touch it, and were so absorbed in it that they did not hear mother calling them to dinner.*

- *dad was very happy to see how all the children liked his idea and also very pleased to see such a beautiful bird so well made.*

- *it could stand there for years and it did.*

19

- under a tap there was a bucket and water was slowly dripping into it.

- pat looked inside and was fascinated by what she saw.

- looking at her, pam knew that she had found something worthwhile.

- she came nearer to the bucket and she too looked at the water inside.

- the three boys who were also in the garden were struck by the look of their sisters so absorbed by the bucket and came in turn to look at what there was to see.

- they all stood fascinated forming a wall around the bucket where the drops of water were producing ripples that would move from the center to the edge one after the other.

- dad came out into the garden and went straight to the place where they were and looked from above them into the bucket.

- he asked them whether they would like to make an experiment.

-they all said, "oh! yes!" as they knew how much fun it was to do things with him.

- *dad turned the tap very slowly so that the drops dripping from it would meet the surface of the water faster and faster.*

- *"do you see how it all changes when the drops follow one another faster and faster?"*

- *now the ripples were seen on the water and they looked as if they were stationary, if the eye did not follow one of them from the moment it appeared to the moment it reached the edge of the bucket.*

- *but when the drops reached the surface faster and faster it became difficult to see the ripples, instead all got lost in water splashing and drops reaching outside the bucket.*

- *dad closed the tap and slightly moved the bucket under it.*

- *now the drops would not fall on the center and dad asked whether anyone could tell in advance what they would see.*

- *they thought hard but no one could guess what they saw a minute later.*

- *when the drops did reach the surface of the water they would make a ripple that was a circle at the beginning but soon was only part of a circle with a new ripple that seemed to come from the edge of the bucket.*

- *"how extraordinary!" said sam, talking first.*

- "turn the tap a little more," said tom.

- "look! look!" said pat, excited by all they were seeing and proud because she was the one who started it all.

- dad told them to repeat the experiment and to watch the ripples on the water carefully as the drops followed one another on it.

- they spent hours at it and enjoyed seeing the circles run away from the center and vanish on the sides of the bucket or come out from them and go to meet other ripples from the center.

- dad was pleased to see his experiment work so well and his children so interested.

20

- pat took the second tooth she has lost this month to mom.

- now she has a big gap in her mouth like many children in her grade.

- she does not mind and even enjoys listening to her esses that now whistle.

- *pam had just gotten her new front teeth and often looked at them as they grew bigger.*

- *tom has one tooth that is wobbly.*

- *everybody apart from tim has had something the matter with his or her teeth.*

- *mom and dad have a friend who is a dentist, his name is doctor brown.*

- *they asked him to visit us and tell us how to take care of our teeth.*

- *when doctor brown came he looked at everyone's teeth and found them strong and white and well looked after and told mom and dad that there was no need to worry, that all the children would have strong teeth and only needed to clean them regularly as they already did.*

- *he also told us that in his travels he found that the people who live in countries where sugar cane grows, have white, bright, healthy teeth.*

- *sam thought, "what a pity that it does not grow in our country, I would prefer sugar cane to toothpaste to keep my teeth healthy."*

- sam asked doctor brown, "in what countries does sugar cane grow?"

- "in warm climates all over the world," answered doctor brown.

- "in fiji too?" asked sam who had read a book on those pacific islands and seen their name on a map.

- "oh yes," said doctor brown, "and much of the sugar cane of fiji goes to australia to be made into sugar."

- "have you been to fiji?" asked pam.

- "yes," said doctor brown, "three times."

- "is it lovely there? is it like our country?" asked pam.

- "it is a group of small islands which are very different from our country, but it is just as beautiful there as it is here and the people who live there prefer their islands to all other places as we do ours."

- doctor brown had to leave, otherwise he would have told us what he saw in his travels all over the world.

- he is a really nice man.

21

- *the five children sat on the rug by the armchair in which dad was sitting, waiting for them.*

- *they had been promised a story and were eagerly waiting to hear him start.*

- daddy said that once upon a time there was a king who had a young daughter called vilnan whom he loved very dearly.

- that child, when she was born, was visited by a fairy who said to her, "I give you the gift of seeing only the beauty in everything."

- when she started seeing, and grew older, the king and queen wanted to know what the fairy's gift was and they took their child everywhere to show her all there was to see, ugly and beautiful.

- but vilnan never turned her face from what to the others seemed ugly: she looked at everything with the same pleasure.

- one day the king announced that he would visit a faraway city and would like his daughter to sit with him and listen to people's complaints.

- everyone in that city was happy to know that the king was coming but was sorry to learn that his young daughter would decide for her father if they were right or wrong.

- the day of the visit arrived and a throne was placed under a tree for the king and a chair nearby for his daughter.

- they sat in their places and the people came to the king with their complaints.

- the king listened but said nothing, leaving the judgments to his daughter.

- she also listened carefully and told the man or woman who was complaining that they were mistaken in thinking that they had been wronged.

- she explained to everyone that they were looking at others only to find what was ugly but that everybody was kind and honest.

- at first nobody was pleased with what she said but because she always said that everybody was kind and nobody wanted to harm them, they started looking at what they were doing themselves.

- they found that if they themselves had been kind and helpful, they would not have found the others so bad.

- they found that often when they blamed the others for starting trouble, it was really they themselves who had begun it.

- the people looked at the young princess with amazement, finding her so young and so wise, and blessed the king for having such a daughter.

- the king now knew what a wonderful gift it was that the fairy had given his daughter, a gift that made her see there is beauty

everywhere and made her want to look at everything for the good it had.

- dad then finished his story of vilnan, saying that another king of a neighboring country heard of her gift and asked that she should marry his son, a nobleman who would become king after him.

- a few years later vilnan married him and together they gave their people the great wisdom of never wishing anything mean and ugly for anyone.

- all children in that land received the same gift from that fairy and became good, just, and generous.

- sam asked dad if that land really existed and pam answered for him that it did not.

- pat and tim wanted to know it from dad, but tom and pam knew that it was a story that could not be true.

- dad then added that perhaps that land did not exist, but he did not know.

- all he knew was that he could think of all of us seeing beauty everywhere if we wanted.

- did they, his children, want to try to see things like vilnan?

- all the five children kept silent, trying to understand what daddy was saying and what it was to have eyes that see like vilnan.

22

- a few days later dad was asked again to tell a story.

- they again sat around him on the rug ready to be taken to some strange land where strange things happened, but dad started like this.

- "when I was a little boy . . ."

- they looked at each other, they never thought that their father had been a little boy and instead of letting him go on with his story, pat asked him,

- "when were you a little boy? is it true that you were as small as sam or tom?"

- dad did not know what to answer, to say "yes" would not mean much.

- so he thought of getting some photographs of himself as a baby and as a boy with his father and grandfather, his mother and grandmother, and other members of his family.

- so instead of listening to a story they all looked at the old album where they could recognize everybody except their father.

- he had to explain everything, where his house was, the time of the day, how old he was then, who was holding him in her arms here, and who gave him that toy.

- when he knew, dad answered, but often he said, "I do not know, I cannot remember."

- the children were very excited to see their big dad so tiny, being taken out in his carriage, playing with sand or some toys that no one made any more.

- they all asked the same questions at the same time and wanted an answer at once and had a new question before dad had finished his explanations.

- for hours they stayed there forgetting that it was a story they had come to listen to and only stopped turning the pages of the album when mom said, "dinner is ready."

23

- at school sam finds much that interests him.

- he loves books and especially travel stories.

- he has a young teacher who has traveled a lot and as a boy read many books.

- so he tells sam what books to take out of the library.

- at the age of nine sam has already looked through all the picture books at school and now he can read some with very few pictures and full of words.

-when he takes them home, his brothers and sisters love to hear him read aloud some of the stories where they find strange names of lands and peoples.

- he has often read to them in the tent with all of them stretched on the mats while he uses his camp bed.

- of course, they prefer daddy's stories but sam comes a good second.

- when sam has no book he cannot yet tell them stories out of his own head, as daddy does, but he has read so many books and so often to them that they know how well he can tell a story.

- they have been taken to africa, to asia, to south america, to islands in the atlantic, and others in the pacific.

- everywhere the travelers have had adventures that make everyone excited when sam reads them and they all dream of being there.

- now they are asking dad and mom to take them on one of their vacations to one of these faraway places.

- dad cannot tell them that such a vacation will cost a fortune, they would not understand, so he tells them, "we shall see."

24

- soon the long vacation, the summer, will be here and for a few weeks a vacation away from home.

- mom and dad have chosen the place.

- it must be in the country because they want the children to be out almost all day, to go for walks and to collect what they can for their nature studies.

- this time they have been lucky for they have found a house with grounds where there are trees, a lawn, a rock garden, a vegetable garden, some beds of flowers, a chicken house, some rabbits, and is not far from the seashore and a beach.

- there are a few country lanes leading to hills, well sheltered, and with no traffic, it will be safe for the children when they go on their own for walks.

- dad showed a map to the children and explained how they will go there in two weeks' time.

- first by car to the station, then by train for three and a half hours, then by car to the house; in all, over five hours' journey.

- everyone is now thinking about the coming vacation, preparing the boxes for the stones, dried leaves, shells, and so on.

- the tent will be sent since it is too heavy to carry.

- the cats will be left behind and the neighbors will look after them.

- everyone is also preparing a suitcase with the summer clothes and all that is needed for one month.

- mom knows that she will not have much of a vacation there and that the children will not help her much either.

- perhaps daddy will.

25

- the journey to the vacation home was long and tiring but nothing special happened on the way.

- tim slept all the time on the train and did not see the many tunnels that they went through.

- in one of them the lights were not switched on and it was pitch black all through.

- only their voices and the feel of mom and dad around made pat remain silent, otherwise she would have screamed.

- fortunately it was not the longest tunnel.

- there were many cows in the fields.

- some of them were looking at the passing train with their eyes wide open.

- in one field there was a young horse, not a pony, small and light on its thin legs, its mother watching, tom called everyone over to look.

- mom gave them something to eat and to drink to keep them in good spirits.

- they had sandwiches, and fruit and orange juice.

- sam looked from the window all the time, watching the landscape and noting the names of the places the train was going through when it was possible to read them, "he missed several which he will find on a map," said dad.

- when they reached the station there was a big car waiting to take all of them and their luggage.

- the driver was a man from this village and so knew all about the route and the countryside.

- sam and pam sat near him and asked questions all the time.

- he always answered them and never told them to stop asking.

- when they arrived he helped them put their suitcases in and agreed to come early in the morning in a month's time to take them back.

26

- the next morning only sam woke up early as all were too tired and slept longer because of the silence in that place.

- sam went out to explore the surroundings.

- he walked round the house first, then looked at the flowers and then at the lawn.

- on that lawn they would place the tent that had already arrived.

- at the back of the garden was an orchard.

- some plum trees full of fruit that would be ripe very soon, and some apple trees, with apples too small to be eaten, were the trees he knew.

- but there were others.

- the vegetable garden had mainly cabbages, cauliflower, green beans, and lettuce.

- he did not see the rhubarb nor the potatoes.

- the rock garden was as lovely as the one at home.

- mother would love that, because it was she who looked after the one at home.

- *it took sam two hours to look at everything and when he returned to the house, breakfast was ready and the others were coming down one after the other.*

- *he ate with good appetite and had two fresh eggs with toast.*

- *everyone had eggs that morning.*

- *afterward mom called them all and told them that she did not want them to make the place dirty, that after playing outside they must only come in from the back and leave their shoes at the entrance.*

- *they had to put their slippers out there so they could change when going and coming.*

- *she also told them that they could not fill the house with what they would bring from their walks.*

- *boxes were to be used and children were to be reasonable.*

- *they all said they understood and would do as they were told.*

- *dad would go with the children on some occasions but they were not to ask him to do more than he could, he wanted to rest first as he was tired from a whole year of working.*

- *but he would plan some longer excursions and tell them about them soon.*

27

- pat and tom had three stones each.

- these were small shining stones they had gathered while walking on the beach.

- one of pat's was reddish, one bluish, and one white with gray veins.

- tom's were much brighter and showed many more colors.

- they only took three each because the day before they took home a large number and mom was not too pleased.

- the house was small and there were so many of them living in it that there was not much room for everyone and still less for stones.

- tom said that he would put the three stones under his pillow and pat found that a good idea.

- "imagine," she said, "if we put all the stones we have under the pillow, what mom will say."

- "she will say that we are mad and she will be right, can you feel your head after many hours on some stones?"

- "the other day I put my head on a rock and it hurt."

- "but you did not put a pillow on the rock," said pat.

- "yes, but the stones will slowly get right through the pillow after a while and wake you up with a pain in your head, neck, or back."

- "all right," said pat, "we will put these stones in our pockets and look at them and show them when we wish."

- *"that is better," said tom, "and we can change them every day for new ones and find more stones on the beach until the summer is over."*

- *when they reached home the stones were in their pockets and their hands were empty, mom did not have to tell them to throw them away.*

28

- pat and pam wanted to start to knit.

- they wanted to buy some wool and make some garments for their dolls.

- mother agreed that it was a good idea and they went shopping one day in a big store to find wool and needles.

- on the way pat and pam asked mother a hundred questions.

- "what needles shall we buy, thin ones or some like those of aunt rachel's, shall we get metal or plastic ones?"

- mother would let them talk and only say, "do you know what you want to knit?"

- if they wanted to knit a blanket for the dolls in their carriages or beds, they would need thicker needles, if they wanted to knit sweaters they must use thinner needles, if they knitted socks they needed still thinner needles.

- but pat and pam were only thinking of buying needles and wool, not of knitting.

- when they got to the shop, they went straight to the wool section and found all sorts of colors and kinds of wool.

- mother let them talk to the salesperson so that they would learn something.

- pam and pat said first, "good afternoon."

- the salesperson replied, "good afternoon, what can I do for you?"

- "we want to buy needles and wool to knit some garments for our dolls, can you show us the needles and the wool."

- "are your dolls big or small?"

- pat did not know what to say but pam answered, "fairly big, like this," showing a distance between her two hands.

- "do you want to knit a dress for the night or one in which to take her out?"

-pat said, "oh! both, and also a dressing gown, a blanket, socks, and sweaters."

- the salesperson looked at mother and said, "they will be busy for weeks knitting all those things for their dolls," and she started showing them different bags of wool.

- *pat chose several, one salmon, one turquoise, one magenta, one royal blue, and one pink.*

- *pam took mostly white ones and some green as she was thinking only of one doll and wanted to knit curtains for her room.*

- *mother asked them to be sure that they needed all that and said that she would let them buy only what they would use.*

- *both said that they were positive, they knew what they wanted, and would knit it all if now mother bought the needles.*

- *they took two pairs each of different sizes so as to have four in all.*

- *mother was pleased by that since it showed that they intended to share their tools.*

- *as soon as they got home they asked mother to start them on their first job and they tried and tried until they succeeded.*

- *when dad returned home with their brothers he saw the two proud girls already beginning to knit a blanket.*

29

- the five children decided to go for a long walk.

- pam and pat held hands and started running, calling the boys to catch them.

- sam wanted to chase them but tim and tom held him by his shirt, telling him not to answer and to stay with them.

- the girls ran and ran until they got tired and stopped altogether.

- they looked in the direction of the boys who seemed far away and thought that it would take them some time to reach them.

- they sat on the edge of the path.

- a few minutes passed and the three boys did not arrive.

- pat got up and looked in the direction from which the boys were to come.

- she could not see them.

- pam got up and started calling, "sa . . am, to . . om, ti . . im," several times.

- there was no reply, only a heavy silence as if the boys had never been there.

- pat said, "pam! do you think they left us here and went together on another road?"

-pam replied, "I think they are trying to be funny, they must be very near here and are not answering so that we will get frightened and they can tell us later on that we have no courage."

- "well!" said pat, "let us not call them but wait until they call us."

- pat and pam on the edge of the path were hidden by the trees and the bushes and hedges.

- they kept silent for some time.

- half an hour later, from very far ahead of them on the same path they heard the voices of the boys calling together, "pa . . am, pa . . at, where are you?"

- the girls began laughing, pleased to have caused the boys to be afraid of having lost them on their walk, but slowly they thought that it would be more fun to be all together and to try to collect leaves, or stones, or any other of the things they met on their way rather than to lose each other.

- so they started calling back and running toward the place from which the boys were calling.

- after a while the five met, tired of running and calling but pleased to be together.

- they started their walk from there, in the direction of the farm at the top of the hill where the miller was so kind.

30

- when they reached the mill they were ready to eat and rest.

- the miller greeted them by name and told them that he was pleased they had come to visit him.

- he gave them a dipper of water that was so fresh and tasted so good that it would have been a good idea for anyone to walk as far as the mill from the valley.

- each in turn drank from the dipper and expressed their pleasure at the freshness of the water.

- tim spilled some on his shirt and was ashamed, the miller took his handkerchief to dry his neck and arm.

- he asked them whether they were hungry and if so to go to his kitchen to get what they liked.

- then he went to his work.

- the mill from outside was like an old windmill but inside was new and modern.

- the miller and his visitors liked to see the wind make these old sails move, and go round with a noise that was both pleasant and terrifying.

- when the children finished eating and drinking they too went into the mill.

- there the miller explained to them how the grain was ground and the flour put into sacks and made ready for the truck to collect once a week.

- *the miller knew that the children were still too young to want to know everything but he took them round and explained all he could and answered their questions as best he could.*

- *pam asked him if he was older than the old mill.*

- *he answered that his grandfather had bought the mill from an old miller who was the last to own it for centuries.*

- *nobody understood what he said but they thought him very nice to tell them all that story.*

- *tim asked him if the grain came from his fields around the mill.*

- *the miller answered that he could grind all the grain in his own fields in one day and that he had work for about two hundred days a year.*

- *again the children did not understand but liked his answer, particularly so because they started dreaming at the thought of two hundred days.*

- *sam and tom wanted to know if the miller had cats or dogs.*

- *he told them that he only had a big dog who was very fierce and he had to keep him in a special room during the day if he wanted to have visitors, but he let him out during the night to watch the mill and the fields around.*

- pam said thank you to him, on behalf of them all, and promised that they would come and see him once more before the end of the vacation and to drink his wonderfully fresh water.

- the miller stayed where he was to see them go and waved at them until they almost reached the gate of his property.

- the children, on their way back, told each other how they liked him and the nice way he had answered their questions.

31

- there was only one week left of the vacation and much to find out about the places around.

- the boys wanted to go far afield but the girls wanted to see more of the nearer places.

- mom was asked to say what she thought.

- she found that everybody was right but told them that since they had been so happy in that place, perhaps they would return there the following year.

- she added that by then they would be stronger and bigger and would be able to go much farther in their walks and perhaps it was better this year to find out more of nearer places than to spend so much time walking.

- the girls were pleased to feel that mom was on their side but the boys were disappointed because they wanted all of them to go for long walks.

- sam said, "today, let us go a long way and see if we like it, if we do not, tomorrow and the following days we can remain nearby."

- pam said, "why don't you listen to mother?"

- "I," said sam, "always listen to mother and have I not said that we shall not go far tomorrow?"

- "yes," said pat, "but only if we do not like our walk."

- tom and tim agreed with pam and pat about sam, but they too preferred to go farther and farther in their walks.

- mom came in again and said, "I think that today you must go in two groups, the boys alone for a long walk, the girls on their own nearby."

- nobody liked the thought of not being together as they knew how much more fun it is to tease each other than to think of what the others are doing.

- at the end tom said, "why not play in the garden today and plan our walks for other days and ask dad what he thinks when he is back tonight?"

- all found that idea better than parting company and they played for hours in the garden.

32

- pat was in bed with her foot in a cast.

- it all happened in the sea when they were paddling near the beach in shallow water and pat's foot got caught in a crack of the rocks and she fell over, spraining her ankle.

- she cried and screamed and called for her mother.

- nobody understood why she was so unhappy.

- but mom held her in her arms and took her to a doctor's house nearby.

- he touched her leg and her foot but when he touched her ankle she screamed with pain.

- he very carefully felt her ankle to find out what was wrong and when he knew he prepared the plaster and the bandages.

- when all was done, he told mom to keep her in bed for a few days.

- pat was pleased to be pampered and when everyone came to visit her, but when her brothers and her sister were somewhere else playing and laughing she would cry and pray that she would soon be with them.

- a week later the doctor called again and took the cast off and put on an elastic bandage, allowing her to join her brothers and sister so long as she did not run.

- as the days went by all became normal and pat even forgot that she had caught her foot in a crack in the rocks.

33

- *sam struck a match and lit the candle.*

- *tim and tom went after him into the cave.*

- *there was water underfoot and the passage suddenly became more narrow.*

- *sam asked them to stop and hold the candle as high as they could so that he could find out whether it was possible to move farther.*

- *when he took a step forward the ground went down steeply and the water rose to his knees.*

- *he told them what he was finding and that it was better to turn back.*

- *tim agreed with him but tom was very sorry.*

- *he was looking forward so much to finding how the cave ended and if there was another opening elsewhere.*

- *still, they walked back as far as it was necessary and soon found the entrance.*

- *the sun was still shining, sam put his shoes to dry and lay on his back on the rocks, tim and tom were looking at the cave and felt sad to have cut their adventure short.*

- *sam said, "let us come again next week with dad and bring with us what is needed to get to the other end."*

- *"what shall we need?" tom started thinking.*

- *"a shovel," said tim, "and rubber boots."*

- *"a flashlight each and perhaps a pickax," said tom.*

- *"a rubber boat," said sam who was imagining that a lake could be found in that cave.*

- *when they reached home later on, they asked dad if he would take them to the cave.*

- *he agreed.*

- *pat and pam wanted to join them but mom said that they would all go together another time.*

34

- in the night, the sky shone with all its stars, each as bright as a light.

- the air was slightly damp and that gave the stars an extra brightness.

- *sam was on his back on the sand, watching one star at a time.*

- *he still felt the warmth left by the sun's rays on the sand and his hand was holding a handful of it and letting it run away between his fingers.*

- *tom sat silently a yard or two from him.*

- *he too was attracted by the silent and immense sky with so many lovely stars shining so bright.*

- *he asked himself, "what are they? are there people living in them who, like sam and me, are gazing at other stars?"*

- *sam said to tom, "are there children like us on those stars?"*

- *tom replied, "why do you ask me that just when I was thinking of it?"*

- *"so there must be people there, otherwise why should we think of it, both of us at the same time?"*

- *tom and sam became silent again and gazed more deeply and more attentively at the sky to receive from it, far, far, beyond the air, some sign of some new friend watching the stars as they were doing.*

35

- the vacation ended and the children were sorry that it had been so short but they really had a lot of fun.

- dad was less tired than when they came.

- only mom could not say that it had been very easy.

- the driver of the car came as promised and helped with the luggage and then took them to the station a few minutes before the train arrived.

- on the platform sam held tim's hand while pam held pat's.

- tom gave his hand to daddy and mom carried the sandwiches.

- the whistle of the train was heard before the train could be seen, as there was a curve before the station.

- they got into their seats and made themselves at home.

- this time tim did not sleep but pat and tom spent most of the journey asleep each in a different corner.

- sam and pam occupied the other two corners and watched the countryside all the time.

- tim stood between them looking out through the window.

- he asked many questions that pam and sam answered except one that dad had to answer.

- the three of them ate their sandwiches while watching and did not tell mother that they enjoyed the chicken in them.

- the day was bright and everything looked lovely.

- as the journey by train was nearing its end mom gave everyone their coat and bag and they were ready a few minutes before they actually arrived.

- the car was there.

- they reached home quite early and found their cats and everything as if they had not left.

- only the tent was not there and for a few days they would miss it.

- sam found a book where he left it, pam and pat took their knitting, tom his stamps, and tim went to the sofa to have a nap.

- mother was preparing lunch while dad was unpacking.

- in a few days' time they would go back to school and back to the well-known life that they liked as much as they liked their vacation.

36

All the children except Tim can read now with small and capital letters. Sam has read many books but Tom and Pat have just started. Pam prefers to listen to other people reading to her because then she can let herself imagine what she hears. But even Pam can now read.

Daddy told us that he is going to give a library card to each one of us if we like for our next Christmas present. We all liked the idea as the public library is not far from our house and on the way from school. "Our public library has a special section for children and a very nice librarian," said Sam, who has already been there.

We can also write and can send our own greeting cards to the family and our friends. When we write we use one script and when we read another, but they are not altogether different, only a few letters are very different.

Tim is not yet learning to read at school but he can tell us many of the names of the letters. He can also read all our names and his. The other day he tried to write Sam's name and everyone read it as "Tom". He could not see how, because he thought of Sam, not Tom. When he wrote "Pam" and "Pat" no one made a mistake and he could not see why we could read these and not the others. He was sure it was our mistake and not his.

Mom leaves us alone when we are studying. She and Dad made up their minds not to help us unless we are really in need. So far we have managed to have a happy life at school and at home. At home we are always together but at school we are part of our classes. At home we talk of everything, at school only of what the teacher accepts and of the lessons. As there are four of us in four different grades we have four of the teachers of that school and we can talk a lot at home about what we did there, but we rarely talk at school of what we did at home. Still, there is more to say about our life at home because there are so many things we do in the tent, and on our walks and outings.

We all like school because of what we do there and we get up early on weekdays to get there on time. Sam gets up early every day because he wants to read or to go out on his own to look at the sun rising or at some flowers in the garden, or to watch a bird he hears. His cat goes out with him but does not return with him unless he is hungry. In the tent, when he is reading alone in his camp bed, the cat finds a place at his feet; if we are all there to listen to his reading, the cat goes out.

37

Pam told Mom one day that she would like to have a place of her own where she could be alone some time during the day. Mom agreed that it would be good if they could find a place for her in this crowded house. The tent is already taken, the bedrooms are already so full that there is no more room for anything. The back of the garden is taken by the vegetable beds and it would not be possible to put up another smaller tent there.

As they were looking at every place in the house and in the garden they both felt that it was impossible for Pam to really be alone in any corner unless the others agreed to let her sit in a room and not disturb her. Mom suggested her own room. Pam would have liked that but thought it selfish as Mom has so many things there she might need in the day's work. Mom said, "Do that and we shall see if it does not work. Maybe we already need a larger house with one room for each of you who are growing so fast." Pam agreed to do as Mother said and was pleased at the idea of having her own room soon if Dad bought a new, larger house. When Pam told Sam what Mother said, he too was pleased to have his own room, but Pat and Tom said that they prefer to have company when they cannot go to sleep and would like to share a room as they do now.

As Pam told Mom that she was now going to be alone in her room, Mom went in and took a few things she needed. Pam felt unhappy, but Mom said, "It is all right, darling; you just retire and be alone as you wish and come out when it is time."

Pam, on her own, looked around and saw how different the room looked now that she would be alone with herself. She did not want to dream, or just count the things on the dressing table, or amuse herself with what the sun was doing on the Venetian blinds. She tried hard to see what it is like to be alone.

At first, she listened to noises and recognized some of them. Others were too faint or too far away to really be heard. She listened to her breathing and was amazed to find how loud it becomes when you do that. She even felt that she was not breathing regularly and tried to change her breathing to make it regular. While doing that she found what it means to be alone. It is being able to watch what matters at the moment and not be distracted by anything else. She was very pleased that she thought of that and grateful to Mom to have provided a place so readily. She would come every time she could to watch what she cannot watch in dreams or in the company of others.

When she came out and went to Mother, her face showed that she had done something she found worthwhile, and Mother knew that Pam would benefit by being alone and she said to her that she would talk to Dad soon about having a new house with one room for each of the children.

38

Pat collects stamps. She does not have very many yet but she has some beautiful ones. At his office Dad gets letters from lands far away and brings home stamps when they are not some he has already brought. His correspondents do not think of varying the stamps they use and he has not yet asked them to do so. Pat begs him to write at the end of his letters: "My daughter Pat would be pleased if you would change your stamps on the envelopes," but Dad has not yet done it.

Among Pat's stamps are some really big ones from Egypt. When she got them she wanted to know all about that country and Pam helped her to find out by borrowing a book on Egypt from the library and doing a search on the internet. They looked at maps online where they found the Nile, the longest river in Africa, that runs through vast deserts and ends up in a delta. In the book it says that the delta of Egypt is made of rich, good land that can have four crops in one year while in our country we usually have only one. On some of the stamps there were pyramids. These are extraordinary monuments where kings were buried. People come from all over the world to see them. On another stamp is a big mosque with two minarets. A mosque is a temple for Muslim people. A minaret is a tower in a mosque from which the people are called to pray. Pam and Sam read and the other children listen and learn.

Dad thinks that it is a very good idea to collect stamps if you also want to learn about the countries from which they come. Of course, Pat now knows many more things about Egypt and other countries than when she started collecting stamps. But what is good too is that all the others at home are learning with her. Think! In a few years' time if Pat has stamps from fifty or more countries and reads books about them all, they will be very well prepared for the trip they are dreaming of.

Dad asked Tom whether he too would wish to collect stamps. Tom replied that he would but he and Pat should choose different countries of the world so that they have two different collections and not the same one. Dad agreed to buy Pat and Tom two stamp albums and to give to them the stamps he gets from the countries each has chosen.

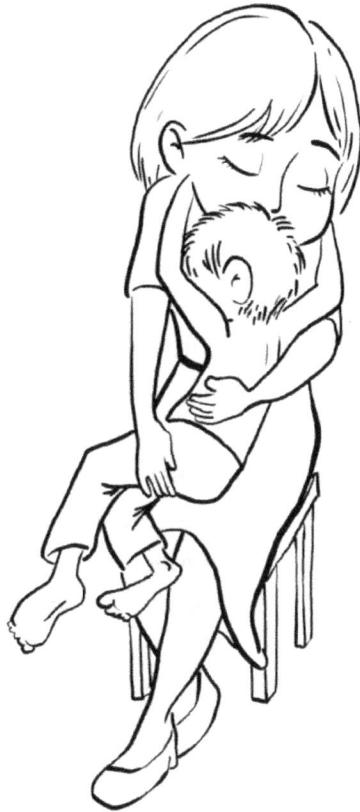

39

On his fifth birthday, Tim received a box of water colors and a fat pad of drawing paper on which to paint. Though he is young, Tim at once liked to use his colors and for hours on end he paints. Mom finds that some of his pictures are beautiful and pins them on the wall of the living room. Every day or so she changes them because Tim finishes each picture so quickly. He loves the bright colors, red, yellow, a special green, and uses them a lot. One day he used dark blue and black only and Mother was astonished. She did not ask Tim why but watched him. As usual he had all his colors in front of him but would not touch the bright colors. He made one picture, then another and another and all were gloomy and dark. After two more pictures Tim went to Mom in tears and told her that he was very sad! Mother tried to comfort him as she usually does and to find out what made him so sad. He finally told her he saw a little cat run over by a car and he had such a pain. Mother knew that it is a terrible thing to see a cat or a dog killed like that and that Tim was sad because he is kind. She said nothing and held Tim's head against her breast until he fell asleep. Tim received from Mother the tenderness he needed to stand the pain he felt. When he woke up he was better and Mom told him a nice story full of colors and of joy and when Tim took his brushes to paint he went back to the yellows and reds and greens.

40

It is Dad's birthday, a very special day for the family. The party is only for the seven of us and the two cats. This is an important difference between our birthdays and Daddy's. We invite schoolmates and friends to spend a few hours in the afternoon and we play games. But for Dad's birthday we do not invite anyone. We do not tell anybody to come because we want to be alone with him. Mom prepares a special cake he likes very much and which he eats only on that occasion. We like it too but we do not ask for it as we let Dad ask us if we want a piece. We thank him very much because he gives us a part of his favorite cake that he will see again only in a year's time.

The party is in the evening when Dad returns from work and we all are allowed to stay up later than usual on that day. Tim will go to sleep earlier and will wake up for the party this year for the first time. Last year it was Pat's turn to be up with us. We sing "Happy Birthday" to Dad and after dinner Daddy tells us a story.

But this year he said, "Mom, you must let your children know that you too were a little girl before you became a big girl and a young woman and tell them where and how we met and you became my wife, their mother." Mom did not know where to start and she was still thinking of the many things that were still to be done that night. She promised that she would tell them when she remembered so many things she had forgotten.

"After all, it is your party," Mom said to Dad. "You either tell them a story or sing them some songs." But Dad said, "When it is their birthday I tell them a story. Today it is my birthday, who will tell *me* a story?" Everyone looked at the others asking "who?" and answering without words, "Not I! Nobody can tell stories like Daddy and who will tell *him* a story?" Dad waited and waited and saw the eyes go round from one person to the other. He was very amused. At the end he said, "All right, I shall tell you a story and after it you wash the dishes while Mom and I sit quietly to rest on this sofa. Agreed?" Sam and Pam were the only ones who could wash the dishes and there were such a lot in the sink. They could not think of finishing it tonight. Pat and Tom were half asleep and Tim had yawned half a dozen times. Mom looking at them said, "Dad, it is not fair to put a condition on your telling them a story. Either you tell them a story and help me wash up or just tell them a story and look at me while I wash up. In fact, let me start washing up as you start your story."

Tonight Dad was pleased with everyone and everything, so he told them a very funny story that made Pat and Tom fully awake and made Tim jump from place to place. Sam and Pam, sitting on the mat with their chins on their knees, laughed so much that their sides were aching. Mom at the sink laughed a lot too and on two or three occasions almost broke a glass or a plate.

As it was getting late Dad ended his story by saying, "Tomorrow I shall go on and you will laugh much more. Now, to bed everyone."

A few minutes later the house was quiet except for Sam's laughter because he was still awake and remembering the funny moments in Dad's story.

www.ingramcontent.com/pod-product-compliance
Lightning Source LLC
Chambersburg PA
CBHW080936040426
42443CB00015B/3436